FREDDRICA NICHOLAS

WHO AM I?

JESUS FIRST ANOINTED DAYCARE

CITI OF BOOKS

CITIOFBOOKS, INC.
3736 Eubank NE Suite A1
Albuquerque, NM 87111-3579
www.citiofbooks.com
Hotline: 1 (877) 389-2759
Fax: 1 (505) 930-7244

Ordering Information:

Quantity sales. Special discounts are available on quantity purchases by corporations, associations, and others. For details, contact the publisher at the address above.

Printed in the United States of America.

ISBN-13:	Softcover	979-8-89391-623-2
	eBook	979-8-89391-624-9

Library of Congress Control Number: 2025906538

Prologue

Who Am I?

Destiny, a nine year old little girl, was an orphan. She was adopted into a home with a loving family at nine months of age. She realizes that her loving adoptive mother and her two sisters and brothers aren't her biological members. Destiny now seeks her identity.

Who Am I?

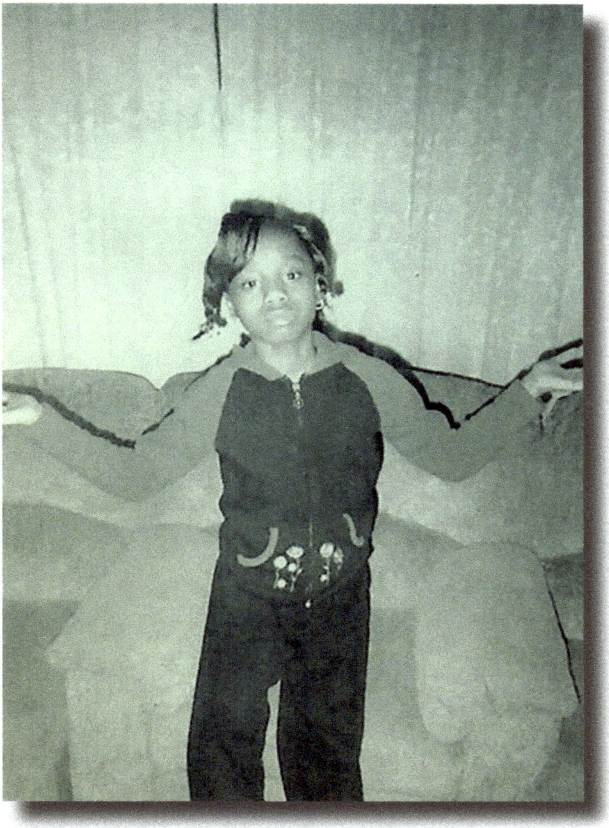

As I look in the mirror on the wall, I am beautiful, bright and tall.

Who am I?

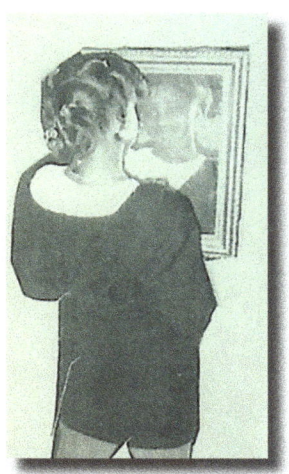 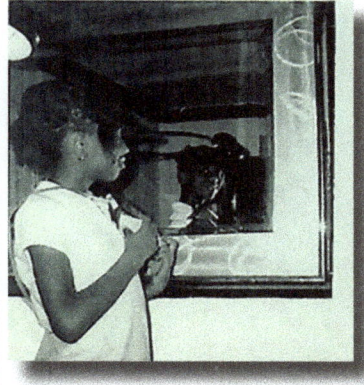

If mirrors can tell you who you are, I'm sure they will say that I'm a star.

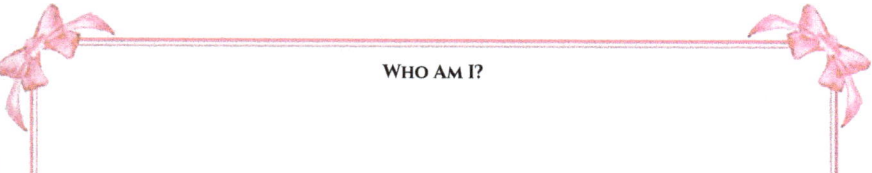

My friends are many: White, black, big and small.
I have fun with them all.

We laugh, giggle, and play every day.

Who am I?

I love to sit and have tea with my family.

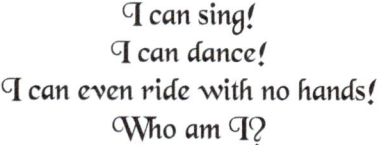

I can sing!
I can dance!
I can even ride with no hands!
Who am I?

My cousin and I like to ride our horses together
when there is nice weather.

My favorite color is pink, I think

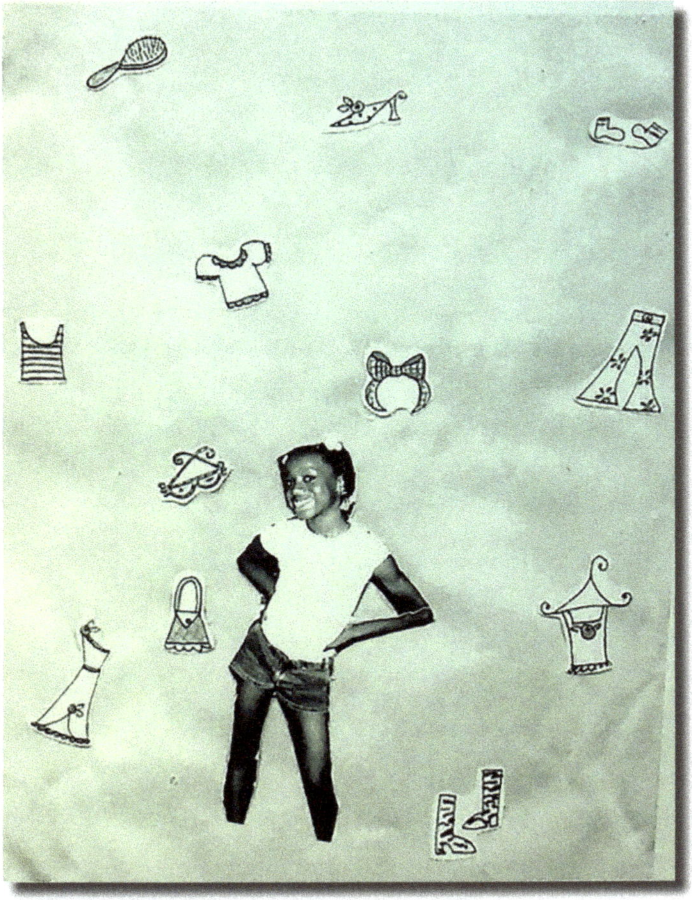

My mother teaches that God created us all just how
He wanted us to be.

I am me!
Destiny.

In loving memory of DestinyNicholas
who gained her wings April 13, 2019